Nude*

*Le plus simple appareil

Anne Portugal

Translated by
Norma Cole

Kelsey St. Press

Grateful thanks to the editors for including sections of this translation in *Série d'écriture, Five Fingers Review* and *Exact Change Yearbook 1.* This translation is dedicated to Rosmarie Waldrop.

Library of Congress Cataloging-in-Publication Data

Portugal, Anne.
[Plus simple appareil. English]
Nude = Le plus simple appareil / Anne Portugal ; translated by Norma Cole.
p. cm.
Poems.
ISBN 0-932716-57-1 (alk. paper)
I. Title: Plus simple appareil. II. Cole, Norma. III. Title.

PQ2676.O727 P5813 2001
841'.914--dc21
2001037993

Cover image: *Odalisque,* 1953–54, by Robert Duncan, wax crayon on paper, 24 × 19. Thanks to Robert Bertholf and the Estate of Robert Duncan.

Book design by Poulson/Gluck

Kelsey St. Press 50 Northgate Ave, Berkeley, California 94708
phone 510-845-2260 fax 510-548-9185
web site: www.kelseyst.com

Distributed by: Small Press Distribution
800-869-7553 web site: www.spdbooks.org

Cet ouvrage, publié dans le cadre d'un programme d'aide à la publication, bénéficie du soutien du Ministère des Affaires étrangères et du Service Culturel de l'Ambassade de France aux Etats-Unis. ■ This work, published as part of a program of aid for publication, received support from the French Ministry of Foreign Affairs and the Cultural Services of the French Embassy in the United States.

Publication of this book was made possible in part by a grant from the California Arts Council and a Hemingway Translation Grant.

for Marc Silvain

Nude

You really know painting
the true distance
stepping back
the cat's eye in the manufacture of marbles
flowerpot to flowers
strong
red of the red bean
you should have a Sugar Daddy even a tired one
even an ugly one
the hereditary symmetry of the rodeo
and its raging desire
to make you dance
whistling to yourself
think think of the kid from Cliff
who relaxes
and lets a crumb fall into your lap
You really know painting

the bath

it is better to know its name
to introduce the scene
by name
it opens onto a meadow

the value of an oath
placed next to green
and the semblance of ease
and of charity

my Susannah
I think is violet
and plump
serious no her first name
in Sweden would be
violent

in Bayeux I posed
a plump woman
under the liberty tree
the blue space between the branches
limned the two elders' heads

she who would take a bath
turning her back on the scene
not feeling where
she connects then I would tell her
that here the two elders would be
frozen really dry and also
their gaze could not
sparkle even if ice
cuts elders' bones to the marrow too

Susannah this landscape suits blondes

because a structure

the bath
can opportunely satisfy
my Susannah
it needs water in it
foreign
rain

(it's out in a meadow)

first activity
the spoon
an associated form
the hoop
do you want Alice
no Sigourney Weaver to
day was breaking
and then the two jokers

no curtain
no curtain

release release   the film titles

what the compressor does
and the rewind which advances
and we who feel it
and the bucket
of tar
to the back
to the back

set your tub there
right where the landing strip
will go

and you stay still the skin has not taken
a sob a wrinkle
Susannah bathing
the title alone protects you
twice
from becoming an elder + an elder
you blush it's a fact
you emphasize the subcutaneous circulation
its wren's
speed
the distance from your heart to your cheeks
must cross a fabulous overcoat
that doesn't cost much at m^3
since it's bath water

turning do you see the only
piece of blue
is never noticed
all in all place
a luggage rack on the edge
of the tub
paint just your toenails
concentrating
interior
modesty
no we are not dead
do you see
and if we blush
that's life
groping along

Susannah is drenched
in the field in Normandy I think
she rules and she's naked
as a blooming apple tree

why such niceties
I set off a mine
Susannah
I prevented nothing
avoid at all cost
the extravagant outcome of mules
and above all the sateen
nightie

and the temperature who really cares
all poems are cold
on the factory-boat

and Susannah is only warmed up
again because she is naked
it's "the closet affair"
which returns to the banning
of fur coats
armor of the fisher king

and Susannah is only warmed up
again because they are old
and they play bullfight
for her play donkey

but in your place

a black woman
for sure
would do it
would create air
in this freezer
convexly
keeping a
lash
on the eye
(but the visitors are
a nuisance)
the glazing
the object B 12 the cramped pose
no running no placing your hand
below your heart
paper flower
23rd parallel
and great pumpkin I think
I understood nothing
to Gauguin

the strongest model
who bends
if he makes a move
who will speak of the raising of arms and the falling
of bracelets all lined up in low country
but not France

oh the dolphin that's cool
that lifts a queenly
ship in less than two
also for your bath
feet swept up
by the bulk
will cover hairy waves
of Venus (her mother)
homologomena knuckleheads
you will return often

it is a vessel borne upon multiple waves

day of rural animation
the beekeepers stir
    like cosmonauts
a kiss for the queen dear dear
dimension of dried bodies

the gold medal ribbon
see Susannah present it to ennui
    to the parched heart

a more familiar animal would suffice
to disassemble
the zzzzzzz's running through her fingers
black water
breeze the zipper made back then

as she lit a cigarette
it happened
that the biggest ashtray she found was the bath

a young man drawing plans
was just her type
there were three

which tossed everything cigarette and smoke
tossed in the air
and kind of laughing

her waist like the potter's wheel
screws on
even the object disappears on the marine horizon

only the moment of feeling
like the others
sweetness of a bit of earth

the exhibition

let us now try to confine Susannah to a rectangle

Bearing in mind that the earth is flat that Susannah is small
and very appealing
and also that the elders look at her from a fixed distance
and that their gaze slides but does not coalesce

if I resolve this problem I could even position myself so
that later Susannah uses a circular tub

the most useful notion here is that of proximity
the gaze beyond the wall
the road lined with lime trees
Annie and the poet
right on time
right
it's the very figure
it's the figure we posed at the beginning of our story

panorama

a nice full length drawing
and sometimes turning
to show that this is a hill
in color
and to reposition the hill
against the ground and then say
it's the same

panorama 1   the bath

Susannah and the elders   exhibition

an arrow "bath water"
then the pink stroke reconstituting details

panorama 2   the garden

title of this picture
"the lovers of the green hill"

panorama 3 the elders

the patch over the eye blocks a corner
oh flattened elder (spinning feeling) on my left
gentlemen with nothing left but skin and bone

panorama 4 the visitors

and the contours
imagine landscape nature
not too interesting
imagine a family outing

oh the valley's pretty face says the girl
standing it's the mountain
and the watering hole trail
not a plane surface you might say says the father
no landscape would sit that way
its arms and its legs
I want to look longer says the mother
I'm going there says the son

panorama 5   Susannah's letters

between two reliefs the table of the seven dwarfs

the green hill's contracted blue veins

panorama 6   the painting

a very famous painting
can always serve as our frame
considering that the exposure
is set in advance
in this case do not move
means
return to the painting
return to the forms
return

now
we have a veritable hearth

between Mobile and Galveston

can Susannah's garden hold as many roses
as Annie's garden

it would be enough to have a dog move
through it
to effect the allées the silence

not that she would look at it

it would be enough that the TGV route
enforce an expropriation
activate the local collectives
to petition

not that she would look at them

basically no visiting
    without palm
thing fixed on forehead
the palm grove
April 1st a blue cup
September 2nd another
            with its saucer
           height of the waves
've started to smile
in apnoea
and I saw your bosom
                blue one time
                 red one time
   yellow another time
cinched
it's an old word bosom
why such severity

in using this very remarkable space
you who pass
my entire body outstretched
and on the bench the bird
one never finds at the same time

it's a temporary exhibit in the provinces

Susannah offers herself a chocolate

from the moment it's mechanically
an accentuation
of the time duration
from the moment it suffices
to fill the morning
floor plan
number of participants
from the moment where it only opens onto moderately
flexible
propositions
participation
experimentation
suggestion
from the moment that on the surface
nothing conjures up a holiday
a particular occasion for saying to oneself oh well then
from the moment it is an endless friction
on plastic brooms
from the moment days pass too
from the moment of indifference
me I engage the city with simple pleasures

now the summer season the need to serve refreshments
in the garden
unmakes
your green and pink face

or else after a certain time

Potiphar is a man and rather
well-built although
of small geometric composition like
the mosaic in the bathroom

Virginie (of Paul and) is
modest
that's to say that a common sentiment
small and blond
or Indian feather
leads her to the edge

her skirts hamper her
her skirts hamper her
her skirts hamper her
Virginie is a girl and rather
obsolete

of the city dwellers none listen knows of Susannah
or her duties
or her significant advantages according to the single version
of which she is the model
brought from Bombay
destined for effects for delay

it seems to me she would hold a red handbag
contained there
in the streambed

it seems to me that red crushed velvet gates
would separate
the field from her side

it seems to me that crows extended on red copper
            feet
keep at a distance
the spectacle's organizers

do you see the beautiful hair that makes the waves
low water
staircase of dying pharaohs

do you want her to hurl abuse at you
it will be in the greatest silence

in your gaze
with her eyes

a huge caterpillar
whose head would have
the regular bulging
and reflecting stripes
and the authoritative look
questioned Susannah

by that confession she had him say
her law of conservation

"the sandbox
me I'm enthralled by that landscape sea view
so short that a pedal-boat hourly rental is
an insane waste we won't even mention a room
by the half-day

in that case cat who laps in turn sticks
a butterfly from behind its throat
in a gesture which puts it in a frenzy backwards
oh would I ravish a grenadier

because I see two hemispheres I imagine
crossing poles
I fly on to Melbourne I feel in a state
of post-sentimentality"

the garden

a second body at night passes

the others watching her the garden gives

amplitude to their sight passes

even the bush it is the tale she gives

do you hear me even in silence passes

a colony of little animals gives

an extra day to live passes

light above all light the taste it gives

so rare he paints leaves gives

the second attempt to erase passes

the hand hours to transfer them gives

strength to the copyists time passes

if one is not named gives

the warning will be given it must passes

the middle of a lovely day gives

tomorrow the weather it is passes

the term for me you know evokes a cemetery
lined with allées that come and go
and on the wall of this garden a figure lights up
cut by the middle of cool October
nights

not ten days will go by
that this heroic composition balances
on the brink of your bathroom
repurchased by the survivors
who say:

oh love in common
in common love oh

that very same day
I saw the sky near
gardens like this
later

on the back of the stone bench
you write your contribution to the tale of the little dog

the dog interested me alot
    the measure of its size
    the two bridges
    over the Seine and over the Eure

the dog interested me alot
    stay across
    in the boat you just
    you will pass just once

the dog interested me alot
    the measure of its size
    toward which
    the bridge of the arch leads

it's not nothing to be this little dog
    red in front
    and blue
    on the ears

it's for its name
for sure that we recognize its gifts its unusual
abilities
Mandrake Veronese's little dog
it's for the double-headed axe
that it knocks in language
it's for the magician
it's for nothing

yesterday came to speak to me
the face
spoke to me

it had not stirred that the room was
organized
for a move

who unfastens me that said from death not a
flag supple in the wind
not a wheel of assistance

the word knee the word window
border pots
insignificant use

my Susannah is sitting in the dark
meticulous red and
green dots
the plane tilts ninety degrees

her chin rests
on a chinrest

her knees touch the knees of the elder
who sizes her up with his right eye
11. 43. 15. in o.p.h.t.h.a.l.m.o.l.o.g.y.

and the light splits the water
panes of glass swimming pools
at five o'clock

the proximate cornea the elder's cornea
from the other side
of red mica
that soon
will be green

her garden encloses trees
fish you recover in the pond
with the moon and her maidens
heaping pebbles

thought meets sounds there
with like grown flowers
that its pallor brings to the grass

a point exists according to the convergences
where elders
register
on folding stools
how she makes her naked arm go
outside

see how she will spend Christmas
accompanied by telegrams of support with a canopy
hung from copper rods
and rings
Apollinaire said of her
scamper and scamper
scamper little mousie

he is virtuous
he looks at his watch
the big hand covering
the little hand
and it's midnight

on this subject of realistic dreams
aptitudes of the instrument the mandatory
dose
and visibility of feelings when it's nice out

like no one working like no one
on a peaceful set
the tongue hanging
"Quiet on the set!"

"PREFIRO ROSAS, meu amor, à pátria"

in the best row perched on aluminum roosts
red-striped
coca cola
voiceless prompters articulate:

M.A.G.N.O.L.I.A.

                                        the “level” by classical
stabilization instrument
suppose
it will be a gala evening a long evening with chairs
the others are going to sing and we
utterly occupied
watching

the right side like when one moves the choice
pages of a book
the other enough in front of one
the profile tracing the shortest path
from the road to the artificial lake

one will speak of nothing

blends

broad authority

realistic black that makes you
the circulation of the blood of others
under the skin

we assure you good company
and if ever your head hangs
over your heart
let's take the big ladder
Susannah will be spotted at four o'clock
in stretch top

and then tomorrow checks and nets

the elders

you remember those verbs appear
seem rest lie
there lie
the gloves
to bear
to the bearer

the ones who lift your skirt bent over so
the map of the anamorphoses
I believe they're watching
the bush that walks
to adjust their sight
to scale

and if they've slipped one across the other
the landscape cuts through their
breadth drying their hearts
scumbled gathering of nights and the most scumbled a fig
tree
on half of the annexed foliage
the blackest character
cut in half
the face
half silent

and at the microscope the one placed his eye
anvil chisel
to examine so big
Susannah's knee in truth
getting bigger

like them passed into the distance through other gardens
and singing when she wished
with a racquet batting kisses to the originals
all alone unit who owns

and the set of points
the sum of x's and y's
the collection
of points to infinity
she was one day authorized
at their intersection

what he sees remains true
strengthens
the proposition
to obey the most natural project

he considers the properties which don't change

in pure variability no figure has known as long as you
how to give change erase the other to attract into the fields
a whole family
look at him
tilt his head back
and be an ass
you will get out you will get out of this anemic hedge
this foliage in its place the crocodile
effect on you of the arrested image

they will age also
even the elders age

I predict to each
a simple death
no looking back
vertical teal blue
beam clockwork
surprise surprise
as if they still wanted to move

by sight you recognize the butchers
by their hands
you tell me how unique it is
to scrape the skin
of animals with a knife

pounded
who is essentially led by
feelings they are serious
they add up the movements
whose sides are not all in the same plane
then hold a conference
caught on his hook

other circle
touching a row of pearl a
window
and men's foreheads
always
set in pairs

fishing tackle
is by necessity
riverside
which is to say they divide
by groups of neighbor
fish
without producing a single dependent
feeling

which looks enough like
gross national product

our boss the earth around
that drives you crazy
it is as quickly often said
that planes crash in the sea

relieved at regular hours
the attendants were astounded
that the garden had no owner
certainly too big
no farmer wood
cutter it might be said a farmyard
for the use of poets ex
clusively serious those
two elders getting
an eyeful please me
relative to wedding bands
the hair the barrette
English figures
curly gentlemen
clergymen constable commodore question
of attitude toward hereditary representation

what looks like cake
’s the share of happiness before Easter
and tomorrow
it will be to revive elder and his friend
elder
departed on ashen feet
both forgetting to look at
the carriage of the freeway-crossing vessel

in the farmyard where you lift your feet
virtuous you
and your gaze of flesh
like today it comes
from poetry
that it be our means of being there periscopically
and our finger on our lips
touched flowed

the visitors

information taken the sign of excellence is not Susannah
what is expected from you
turn your face towards us
tell us

"as I did not know the comings
of their goings
in the snow
that with chocolate the smegma disappears
I was feeling alone collecting
provisions
for winter
the great expeditions

that prepare for the next stage
stealing from the community
now
she wants so little
that to see
a drama
a display of lemons
General Custer's sword
in motion
innoculates her greatly
justly he moves
he glues
he rips he stacks
he climbs the ladder
he moons
greatly

which compromises the lesson of things"

“For me stops me
the gaze
that guy there
exposing himself

and the old white gaze
is enough

or if you want to work harder
          let’s focus more aggressively
on the basis of the sausage-maker’s activity

deprived
of his iron
frame
if a steer
becomes
sumptuous
by placement of ownership
by singular
apparition
in the middle of the night
premise
of a new stake
of absolutely
clean
origin
are you recording this
like a novelty?

your eyes hastily
magnetized
it’s love
it’s love
that guy
exposing himself”

look at us Susannah
tell us

“his name wrapped
in rope in string
like concern
gangrene
                        and his lightweight legend
intervening I am quoting only at times
of current ambitions
and the vast operation of his laughing thus
the window washer
on his ladder
polishes
the pane
and I recognize him there an equivalence
without sparkle”

look Susannah
tell us

"bully the condition
of belly up
no matter that your coat be spotless
it attracts the laying on of hands
fleeting
petunia
that supports petulance and tobacco
the boss's babe
had monkey fingers
at her fingertips

he threw himself upon me
Mister Commissioner
accompanied by a veritable decoration which was
the belt
and because it cost the price
and because it had associative
functions
like yourself I support the guilty
any time
I never stop myself from laughing at that"

there there the parade of providers
and the row of places visited by whole families
Sunday
the grass yellows
in the apartments

“I am speaking in time x
on tape
into the mic
to the axe
to silence

all — of you whom I look at with my eyes
each one — inspired by the mountain
all — of you I simultaneously paint
each one — swayed by the ocean in your bathing suit”

respect the timing of visits

there there the parade of providers

the hairdresser has his combs
he appears within
fresh
mint
        Gerard
or Chrisostome

to his lover
who is canoeing
above
the dam
he offers
some pledge

Friday
he rushes the cuts
a little
he appears
very fetching
the day he resumes

there there the parade

four sewermen
four boys amazingly barded with spice
and big and strong real heavy breathers
which highly elevated
their zippers

together they spoke to each other of tactics of
now's the time
to pull the ladder up

together they held their
feet on the high rungs

there there

on the slanted garden
a slant a public
garden
which makes the two Paris gardeners
look like
mural
allegories
to that as close as to the slope
they cling like mountain
cows
be it vertically and almost
giving in
to their mutuality

which makes the height of the boots on each leg
proportionate
to the boy's bending
to pluck a seasonal
flower
that shakes its root at him
steady at house
level
if the boys gather bunches
of flowers
it's to save them
from wilting
on the mayor's
orders
the two boys

the restricted word

it was agreed upon that a certain distance would be
kept that girl
subscribes
to the cement factory
she is charming

on the right a palm tree
Montcalm and his smoke

on the left the fly
adept at circulating

she learns the exclusive application of their eyes on her skin
of the map of living happily
of thumbs up

above
nothing
appears at this hour timely

no going back up there
a hundred grenadiers by the window
is a lot
but a little regiment
that knocks on
the pavement
is pleasing
to neighborhood residents

every shack has its girl-next-door
and the surge of photographers
or maritime observers
marks their scores
above the painting

needed are two twins
two horsemen
to cross the zone

came alone
unaware
and in the minefield
crossing with nothing exploding
unaware
clogs near the detonators
and the denser fine gravel

but when the visitors reach her level
everyone stops
and looks at Susannah

she's put on weight she's put on weight
it's impossible believe me
eternity does not
carry on like this

she holds on her knees
two impoverished hands
in a mirror
with her teeth
she winks
for the sun only waits
to dedicate
the whole
to white marble

(whispered)

someone tells you her name is Madame Aubain
for the reason
that she is from Normandy
so she's seen the valley of the Sienne
empty out at the bottom

(Madame Aubain was not by nature expansive)

that this relation occur at low tide
a thigh a leg of lamb
it is not she
it can not be she
she
can not cover up this concept of exhibition
but yes her indifferent
maid
whose profession it is to pose for the baptism
    of our Lord Jesus Christ

Susannah's letters

"seen from over here
there was this man whose profession
is taking the dead from their apartments
he looked at me so civilly
so alert into his gaze intelligence slipped

I need said Susannah to write his name
I need said Susannah to take him these letters my stations

chronicle of a year of misery

pardon this bath
is livable all year round
even if the heart (need beat no more)
leaps and leaps in the air
why I stay on the edge of the pool
why I stay"

Yours truly

lovely eye who ever
you are silence
carries the furniture
to your door
and all the mountain
when one sees it
past wrongdoings
hurt no longer
even the hall
is covered
in gold buttons

and when a man is sensitive
somewhere in his spirit
he also is in love

Seen from over here

from the horizon there
is an unavoidable
acceleration of the
heart toward the night
one does not wish for
other passages
toward other lights
and if we can
you see the trouble believing
you see the words
the movements
as soon as they're created
by mouth

and on the evening questionnaire
one crosses out
descriptive entries

Seen from over here

            from the passage lit
by flames one would see
a barque cover
a barque
because the night
and the back
the water presses them opposite
to stretching out the neck there completely

and review in full
the chapter on
the sinner's conversation

Seen from over here

        diorama
gathered sixty winegrowers
be done with it for God's sake
come to the table
a lovely day
at least it needs
to be something
that looks like them
simple mirrors
in the sink's reflection

and the first to wear the medal
he sees himself
in the sky's beginnings

Yours truly

lynx hotel
a cigarette with the mushrooms
a card
at 1/100,000th
touching the emptiness face
doctor B. look me
in the eye tell me
if the menu
seems okay
for it happens that the longtime
lack of definition
incurs general censure

a mist
in the lowlands
a paste-up façade

Seen from over here

            from the belvedere
Ottavio would spend
most of the day
framing his eyes
with a straw
the bar's chipped
plates bring
him upright
with the same pipe
the same quicksilver

and much beyond
and me
the unforgiving

Yours truly

watchtower hotel number
twelve the key
in a bowl
and the dust
raised
doing something to oneself
it looks like you can
open the windows one
with one thrust
the other
not so sure

and since you are leaving
you are invisible
but only after

Seen from over here

modern you do not
change feeling
in the annex
you pass plates
according to
the orders
now it feels like
return trips to the kitchen
cold leftovers
a spiral
around a cone

and who has seen him ill
so well-behaved
but not childlike

Yours truly

the beau rivage what we
call "living" room
opens on the blonde
upon whom weighs a pound
of flowers the grocers
drink wine not
looking at the trim
the trunk's iron fittings

and the sky's light
falls in little copper
jets

Yours truly

lighthouse hotel it
snowed yesterday
which did not
disturb
the chambermaids' floor
it did not
reach 5
the thermostats
in the rooms
they will be cold

and on the same order and by the same order
the nakedness of a corpse
or the circumference of the circle

Seen from over here

panorama it was
a frontal
ceremony it rained
the silver ring
balanced on
the table with that
he would marry her
and even saint john
like red pepper
the leaves stick
to his eyes

and how everyone thinks
everything is in order the tree-
lined avenue

Yours truly

hotel miramar sleeping
once under your name
I let down
the yellow curtains
the symmetry
of the sun
did as much
the window appeared
wide

and heart view of Jesus sudsy
bullet stuck with silver
badge of Royal Canadian Mounted Police

Yours truly

    from Nevers
the Easter wine is black
there is a green
and blue cover on
the mantel
on the count of three
the strong will
be traded
for the weak
air in the hands
claps at the counter
a sound of cash
register

is it your will
and if I were over there
enveloped in lifting

Yours truly

Bellevue fixing a belt
on the edge
on the balconies vertigo
construction of the sky
never a fantasy
does not come after noon
to disturb
the core of the sad
egg

and if the crowd advances
such slow movement of the dresses
doesn't count

Yours truly

Beauregard closed
in the morning eyes
by the smoke
united with carbon
thunder
he got away again
the upright man

and coatless the lamb
passes from yellow to green
and not laughing

Yours truly

hotel excelsior behind
the door read the winter
prices the summer prices
and the difference
binds the heart
it's authority alone
which can enlighten us
a hoop around
the basin
and the fish

and to enter the common room
you reinhale
all the air in the world

Seen from over here

the forest
touching dead bodies the head
solid
and transparent the encounter
with them with
those others that they recall
that one could increase them
until they equal
a property extending
as far as the interstate

and it is not a detail
that certain ones
are never satisfied

Seen from over here

vast general slumber upon the pigeonholes
beside
the numbers darkness
and in a few seconds
the intention of
ordering a chilled
drink and on this hope not counting the wait
by this letter
and by all that holds
as if outside the world
it is raining

and what that problem is
where are the small numbers
where are the large ones

"yes I was gazed at by that unhappy knight
whose fearsome goodness
brought answer to my enmity"

I told him that I loved loincloths
and virtue
that meanwhile I preferred vertigo
and that silly
climbing the cardboard
mountain's rock-face
and falling in the water splat
into a Canadian canoe

from the shepherd it happens that a single letter
stamps the shepherdess
because she weighs a gram twice
her weight in powder on earth

thus all flying things enhance the symmetry of the double
the messenger's legs
above our heads

demonstration by the mediation of a crest

one knows they are playing their queens
by the knucklebones' shadow cast on the wall
see them turned over
and figure 1 pictures an imminent journey
and figure 2 the traveler

the painting

material points will always be considered like
perfectly elastic links think
boxers
gradual increase of force
in flight everything brings us back
and the painter
to his model
and the painted canvas
despite a lively experimentation

to represent the world in parallel planes
pierced by an arrow
points of contact ab bc cd de ef
wounds
all arranged on the diagonal

the landscapes of the day are looked at piecemeal
differently
from the neighbor
and if he chooses to cut out
the other hedge
he's pleased by
the other hedge
compassion attracts him
to the other hedge

then to alter the body without thinking
of the ladder
by a hair to avoid the curse
of passage and the painter
with seductive crotch
in bermuda triangle
offers the household instruments
of the northern dwellers

if the wind whistles
if it is fair to the whistler to count one two three
so passionately not at all
of whom it concerns laughing and making a big display
nothing comes
nothing makes a greater effect than smoke signals
from the catadioptric Indians

what makes some nests some voids
hides without hiding that it contains
a building
what you drink
with rooster
powder
embarrassed or finishing
by stopping the ladder
right at the edge of the sidewalk

swinging games
swing
at this
height
engaged
your wings swing
your beaks leap
into the air

in order to meet again Susannah
you must discourage the inspectors

in a kiss the afflicted
pose
the honest
pose
to foresee an infinity of collisions
operation angelic smile

set with wheat with lovely lovers
you would need this certain Ceres
and in order to say it
their lips tickle
blending a heavy sob
of welcome with your goodness

oh the young man is sweet as
an unmated the gentle rising slope of the wave
is going to break

I don't know
if it's
the spirit of wash-my-feet
the leap in ladies' hearts
on a donkey ride
and who provokes laughter
or else
the day so blissful fine

it's still you surprise
in camouflage outfit

at this moment seventy-eight pigeons overtake the Paris-
Ventimiglia express
you reread *The Ravishing of Lol V. Stein* just the cover

it's a practice of an unbelievable thinness and mornings
the maker of hosts makes them flatter still and almost
transparent

there on the grass court your skirt is white and short
ah I feel nothing in the air of your whereabouts
in the passing of seed

are there others besides you in this garden
the worker would ask
ever with her lamp

oh but that is of no importance
for getting plot points
that occurs by itself
by sight
and memory bakes it for a million years
the few bars of chocolate from childhood
add up to nothing
that fits better than a tomb
than a shoe beneath the elbow
and the sigh of the candle amuses me
in full knowledge of the case
for I come at the same time
to open and close
the circuit breaker

Susannah queen of Egypt
current version
according to which
they bring back to the Channel's shore
an ailing
little sister
who dies
in a few days

come he knows it she's silent
her flocked wool
waist shrunk
to meet 007 Susannah the dwarf

On a wooden base from the islands
Unity of gaze unity of gaze
Zarcos & Co. airmail export
African so rosy so strong Loretta
Do not show off your death spit in its eye
Black this swimsuit this cankered
Collar the drawing of a flame mi
Ssion accomplished james and all that jazz
Once said she smiled
Zohra the pastor's wife who liv
Ed a lovely adventure...

Naturally it will be necessary to
Feed them to lure them with meat
And vase verses *fifises* in the sun

problems with debt it seems
on a boat
the distance from my life to your life
shrinks

gun range has no longer course
and the planes toss
lose altitude
smoothing our Indian heads
dressed for the farewell ceremony

a few strokes to get out of the painting
customs vehicles immobilized
sabotage

the whole length
of sidewalk is blocked
abundantly
flowered
with little words
encouraging
informants

momentary drunkenness of the whole garrison

Susannah escapes Susannah flees
the swinging of arms increases the kinds of waves
closure
one took that into account
in the manner of mounting large horses
of lifting the guts

it's only a gallop of sheep filled with bone

little American photo

you run into her again on earth
in the company of two young worn out
smiling
not very intelligent

and since the sun is not low enough
she squints looking at the beige motorbike

simply on a line the whole length
Susannah hugs her knees
dream twice as strong
that she's Marilyn

with the opera glasses
you see
a sentinel remains
and the same still in that place
will recognize Susannah in chilly
plaster
sitting on the other bank
look here is my bed covers
the voice which engages her
to get back to this woods

they'll say they've seen the pyramids
that sand or mica
moves the outer parts of their vision
in order to go forth
knees pass with feet
familiar evolutions
they'll say they've seen the pyramids

who returns back to the stage
would not greet
would not take care still to please
would sit between the two elders
and would weep
eye patch
in advance lost again

we learn by this operation
what will be
the following experience

the enjambment of celestial bodies

a weight of intensity
thick
as the air

visibly your planted
foot
and your lateral thumbs

lifted could not
contain
emotion when it changes in pain

we have seen that the places on earth in general
occluded
and when one is within

diverge from the subject of air

and to notice you
it's the last thing
they thought

that you were balancing in the air

the maybug will become a mouth
at the height
of the flower

thus the woods suspended will act

and the distance to the sun
shortening
your hitching post

like they do with fuses
will get
disassembled

your polished astronomical
body
it will be seen perhaps sinking

an hour after
it will
rise

with the weight of the supremely frozen air

no force created and by that instrument
the telescope
they believed

and by the application of force
they were
applied

to reduce the proportions

no one laughs
at following
all the effects of you

for the naked eye
will surprise
it's simple

the alignment of your indifferent thoughts

when we turn back Susannah towards Rosemonde's palace
speed will be a positive number
the treetops will attain a lovely proportion

and so that nothing gets the soldier
killed in your place
you will lift your eyes before the collision

we who speak of wall and of garden perimeter

when we turn back Susannah towards Rosemonde's palace
in a bad departure position tired
the crowds and we
that nothing will stop us
from speaking to you to who speaks
of you to speak louder
than the wall you agree
and you speak to the absentees

when we turn back Susannah towards Rosemonde's palace
we two that nothing stops us
and the garden will be criss-crossed by arrows
we won't dodge
and you will tell this story:
and so a man sets out at point zero